INTERIOR CONSTRUCTION DOCUMENTS **WORKBOOK**

Katherine S. Ankerson

FAIRCHILD PUBLICATIONS, INC.
NEW YORK

Executive Editor: Olga T. Kontzias

Assistant Acquisitions Editor: Carolyn Purcell

Art Director: Adam B. Bohannon

Director of Production: Priscilla Taguer

Production Editor: Amy Zarkos

Editorial Assistant: Suzette Lam

Copy Editor: Amy Jolin

Interior Design: General Meador, Inc.

Library of Congress Catalog Card Number: 2003102031
ISBN: 1-56367-254-5

GST R 133004424

Printed in the United States of America

Contents

Preface

The intent of *Interior Construction Documents* is to promote an understanding of the manner in which the fundamentals of a set of construction documents are developed and assembled. The text and workbook provide an opportunity to understand individual construction documents' components and elements, their beginnings in the design process, and their relationship to each other and to the project as a whole. It is written to assist students in gaining an understanding of the philosophy, content, order, and relationship of construction documents as well as the development of each portion.

Interior Construction Documents provides information, integrating a variety of learning experiences and approaches to assist the student in internalizing the information. Animations are provided that illustrate various processes involved in the development of construction documents. Animations also direct the reader's attention to particular areas of emphasis in a sequential manner. The animations and illustrations are an integral component of the text and must be viewed or experienced, in addition to the reading, to achieve the level of understanding intended. The learning experiences designed and included in this work include the illustrated text, audio text, animation and simulation sequence clips, annotated details, and drawing examples. The workbook is designed to promote a deeper understanding and allow application of the information learned. The text may be heard by activating the audio component. Adjust the volume on your computer as appropriate. When opening the CD-ROM for the first time, you are encouraged to check your system for the minimum program requirements. Installation of required players are provided on the CD-ROM.

Examples presented herein are done so for illustrative purposes only. It is neither expected nor recommended to use details or design solutions out of context. Each detail, plan, elevation, section, schedule, and specification section is related to a particular condition and must be customized to meet the project requirements. *Interior Construction Documents* presents examples of portions of construction documents in a

NOTES:

_____

_____

_____

_____

_____

_____

_____

_____

_____

_____

_____

_____

_____

_____

_____

_____

_____

_____

_____

_____

manner that relates the act of creating a construction document to the final result. *Elements of Interior and Lightframe Construction*, by author Katherine S. Ankerson, is a text that covers aspects of the components of construction that must be understood to create a quality set of construction documents.

Disclaimer

The information in this text is presented as a result of many combined sources, including interviews with current design practitioners, interactions with contractors, review of building and fire codes, review of common reference books and standards, and the author's professional experience. A list of suggested reading is included for further information on a number of subjects related to construction documents.

Even though the author and publisher believe the information presented to be accurate and complete, they do not warrant it as such. The author and publisher have attempted to make this book as accurate as possible, but do not warrant its suitability for any specific purpose other than as a teaching and learning tool; and they assume no liability for the accuracy and completeness, or the application of the work to individual circumstances.

It is the responsibility of users to apply their professional knowledge in the use of the information presented in this book. In no case should the examples provided in this text be used without the express written consent of the author. The reader should consult and follow manufacturer's literature in the selection and application of any specific products.

NOTES:

NOTES:

_____
_____
_____
_____
_____
_____
_____
_____
_____
_____
_____
_____
_____
_____
_____
_____
_____
_____
_____
_____
_____
_____
_____
_____
_____

Acknowledgments

A desire to increase effectiveness and power of learning tools for students and educators in interior design was the impetus for this project. A unique combination of my professional education and experience coupled with a willingness to explore the educational possibilities offered through technology has shaped this work. To that end, each interaction with other design professionals, contractors, and students through the years have in some manner influenced the material presented here. I extend my appreciation to students at the University of Nebraska, whose quest for understanding, knowledge, and excellence have been a source of inspiration.

My colleagues in interior design education have provided both encouragement and inspiration. Contemporaries associated with other academic fields, yet with a profound interest in tapping the power of technology as an educational tool have been a stimulus, and I have learned much from them.

Kevin Tedore has been a joy to work with on this project. He has transformed my sketches, images, drawings, and ideas and given them an active digital life. His suggestions have been valuable additions to the navigation and artistic quality of the digital work.

Without those in the profession who have so generously shared images, video interviews, and drawings for this text, relevance to current practice would suffer. Bradley Milton, principal with RDG has provided exceptional support through project examples from the initial sketches through professional photography of the final product. He has provided valuable advice to the work as well as his thoughts in video interviews. While the professional practice of interior design may claim many similarities, the field is diverse. Bradley Milton, Paul Hagle, Carol LaMar, Becky Kiedow, Amy Cassell, Jeff Day, Christiana Wachal, and Phillip G. Bernstein, FAIA, have each lent rich diversity of perspective to particular issues regarding construction documents. Readers will benefit from the collective experiences and wisdom of these professionals. Design firms have graciously and generously contributed work for this text. I am grateful to

NOTES:

_____

_____

_____

_____

_____

_____

_____

_____

_____

_____

_____

_____

_____

_____

_____

_____

_____

_____

_____

_____

_____

_____

_____

_____

_____

_____

AutoDesk, Duncan Aviation, Gensler, Mossien Associates, OWP/P Architects, and RDG for their contributions. Carl Matthews, Roberto Rengel, Vivian Lee, Bruce McCawley, Teri Neruda, Eunseok Cho, Melissa Martinez, Melissa Kleve, Trisha Atwood, Sheila Lammers, Kelly Dubisar, and Erin McCawley each supplied examples of work for this text. Without the contributions of these people, the text would have suffered tremendously.

Olga Kontzias, Amy Zarkos, and Carolyn Purcell at Fairchild Books are an author's dream. Their enthusiastic support and ready availability are appreciated. I would also like to thank the following reviewers for their insightful advise: Glenn Currie, The Art Institute of Pittsburgh; Donna Weaverling Daley, Daley & Jalboot Architects; Attila Lawrence, University of Nevada—Las Vegas; Luann Nissen, University of Nevada; Jill Pable, California State University, Sacramento; Marty Plumbo, University of Cincinnati; Christopher Priest, Minnesota State University; and Roberto Rengel, University of Wisconsin-Madison.

Finally, I wish to extend my acknowledgment and appreciation to my family for their support. Through the encouragement and support of my parents and my husband John and children, Jason, Matt, and Kelsey, this work has been nurtured from seed to a healthy existence. They have shared the vision.

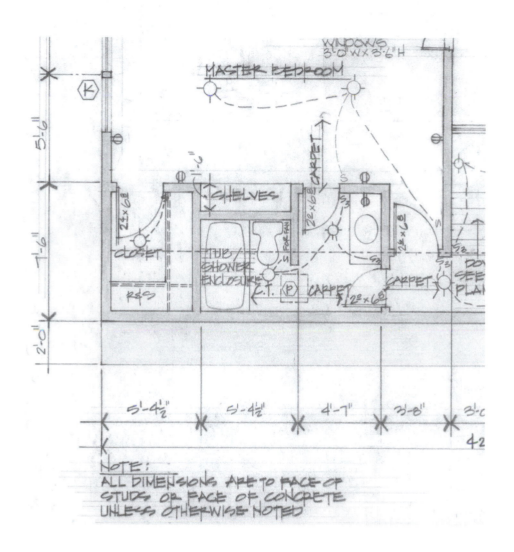

NOTE:
ALL DIMENSIONS ARE TO FACE OF
STUDS OR FACE OF CONCRETE
UNLESS OTHERWISE NOTED

CHAPTER ONE
Philosophy

Construction documents are created to communicate a design project to contractors for pricing and ultimate construction. As such, they serve as instruments of the legal contract between the owner and contractor. Designers have an obligation to the owner of the project to provide accurate, consistent construction documents that describe the project agreed to by the owner and designer.

Projects designed may vary significantly in the scope of work. Each aspect of the project must be described in a coordinated and related manner. The construction documents include drawings, schedules, and specifications as an interrelated whole. Large projects may contain more in terms of the volume of information, but all projects contain similar types of information on construction documents.

Industry standards provide a common language for this communication in the manner of accepted order of drawings and specifications, common abbreviations and drawing symbols, and drawing conventions. Within these standards, a wide diversity of approach by individual firms to the preparation of construction documents exists. This diversity often stems from the firm's basic philosophy of service but may also stem directly from the wide array of project types and sizes encountered in the field of interior design.

Construction documents provide clear, complete, and accurate communication regarding the design intentions of a project. Some information is best communicated in a graphic form, while other information is most clearly communicated in writing. The integral nature of construction documents suggests that a combination of graphic and written material be used to describe the project fully.

Drawings in a set of construction documents illustrate the extent, size, location, and relationship of elements to each other and to existing building components. Drawings are in the form of plans, elevations, sections, details, and sometimes axono-

NOTES:

_____

_____

_____

_____

_____

_____

_____

_____

_____

_____

_____

_____

_____

_____

_____

_____

_____

_____

_____

_____

_____

metrics. Each of the drawing types is uniquely suited to convey specific types of information for clear communication of the condition.

Drawings are supplemented by schedules that describe the type, finish, and location of materials or objects. Schedules provide a link in many ways between drawings and specifications. They are used to record great amounts of information in a small, easily referenced space.

Specifications in a set of construction documents focus on workmanship, allowable tolerances, and standards of quality in materials and installations. Specifications may be included in a separate book, often referred to as the project manual. There are many types of specifications that may be created depending on the scope and bidding processes for the project.

A common message describing the project and its details must be present in the construction documents. This common message is reinforced by consistent and coordinated drawings, schedules, and specifications. "Common message" refers to the overall description of the materials, components, and construction of the project. The point of creating an accurate, clear, and consistent set of construction documents is to eliminate the presentation of conflicting information which may lead to change orders, misinterpretations, and potential project changes.

Designers have the responsibility to interpret client needs, to create quality designs, and to communicate those designs in a manner that allows the project to be successfully constructed. It is important to create a complete and accurate set of construction documents because they form the basis for contractual obligations between the owner/client and the contractor.

Responsibility to the profession in regards to construction documents refers to upholding high standards of communication and taking responsibility for informed decisions. Designers also have a responsibility to know and follow relevant codes for the type and location of the project. Interior designers have an ethical responsibility to the client to represent an accurate and full description of the approved design as a set of construction documents. The client relies upon the designer's specific expertise and judgment.

Construction documents provide the vehicle for communication of the designer's intentions (based on the client's needs and desires) to the contractors for construction. The construction documents consist of drawings, schedules, and specifications as an interrelated entity. These documents become the basis for a contractual relationship between the client and contractor, and, as such, must be accurate and complete. This chapter covers the role of construction documents within contract documents as a whole; the importance of accuracy, clarity, and consistency in their preparation; the interrelationship of the interior designer's portion of the construction documents to other design disciplines; and the responsibilities of the designer in the development of construction documents.

NOTES:

Name:

_____

Investigation of the actual codes in force in a particular jurisdiction is a very important step in beginning a project. This investigation typically occurs prior to the Schematic Design Phase.

Complete the blanks to the right with relevant and current information regarding building and life safety codes in the jurisdiction in which you live.

Assignment # 1

Authorities Having Jurisdiction:
(Name of city, county, or other jurisdiction.)

_____

_____

Codes Information:

Building Code: _____

Building Code Edition: _____

Life Safety Code?   Yes   No   If yes, edition: _____
(Circle one.)

Other codes, regulations, or standards in force:

_____

_____

_____

Code Official's Name: _____

_____

Code Official's Phone Number: _____

_____

Name:

_____

Place a mark in the box to indicate which portion(s) of the contract documents the described information would be found.

Assignment #2

Contract Document Components	Generic elaborations on portions of the owner-contractor agreement	Project price	Description of the specific materials to be used on the project	Changes during the bidding process	Changes during preparation of construction documents
Agreement between owner and contractor					
General and Supplementary Conditions					
Construction Documents					
Modifications					

Name:

_____

Fill in the blanks with the most appropriate term or name.

Assignment #3

A. _____ are used to organize and communicate large amounts of information in a small space and serve to bridge between information found on drawings and in specifications.

B. _____ is the portion of construction documents that focuses on workmanship, quality of a product, and allowable tolerances for installation.

C. _____ is the portion of construction documents that portrays graphically the extent, size, and location of elements within a space.

D. _____ and _____ are the professional organizations who have developed standard forms of agreement for use by designers on projects.

E. _____ is the organization responsible for developing a three-part format for specifications.

F. The sequencing and coordination of subcontractors during the construction of a

project is the responsibility of the _____

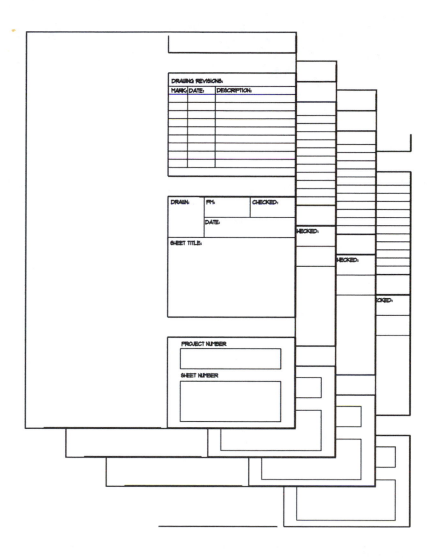

_____

_____

_____

_____

_____

_____

_____

CHAPTER 2
Content and Order

_____

_____

The nature of construction documents prepared by the interior designer will depend upon the scope and type of project as well as the projected method for construction bidding. Enough information must be communicated about the project so that the client, designer, and contractor understand the full scope of work in the same way. Regardless of variables that may affect the amount or type of details included or the depth or type of specification used, there are some basic premises on which the content and order of construction documents is approached.

Order of information in construction documents is important when creating a new set and also when searching for information regarding an existing building. Designers must know where to locate relevant information on construction documents for existing buildings. The information in a set of construction documents for a new building must be consistently placed and easily locatable.

Anything that will be built, attached, or is in some way a permanent part of the building is typically described as a part of the architectural series in construction documents. This is the case regardless of whether the primary design professional is an architect or an interior designer.

An A at the beginning of the sheet number designates the architectural series within a set of drawings. Site work (designated with a C for _Civil_) and structural work (designated with an S), as well as mechanical (designated with an M or P) and electrical work (designated with an E), are each described in separate portions of the construction documents that complement the architectural series. Furnishings are shown as a part of the interiors series of drawings (designated with an _I_).

An entire set (including architectural and interiors as well as all of the consultants) of complete construction documents for the construction or alteration of a building will contain drawings designated by letter according to the appropriate series and arranged in a particular order.

NOTES:

_____

_____

_____

_____

_____

_____

_____

_____

_____

_____

_____

_____

_____

_____

_____

_____

_____

_____

_____

_____

_____

A significant amount of information is relayed about the design through the construction documents. This information is communicated through drawings, schedules, and specifications. To be the most useable, searchable, and communicative, the information must be organized in a logical fashion. Organization and presentation of information on construction documents has followed various formats over the years.

A recent push to standardize the organization, sheet content, and file naming conventions for drawings and schedules has resulted in the form of the Uniform Drawing System. Specifications are typically arranged according to the Construction Specifications Institute's (CSI's) 16-part format.

Name:

_____

In the space to the right, describe four major factors that may influence the preparation of construction documents, giving an example of each to illustrate your understanding.

Assignment #1

A. _____

_____

_____

B. _____

_____

_____

C. _____

_____

_____

D. _____

_____

_____

Name:

_____

Utilizing the sheet designation method suggested by the Uniform Drawing System, indicate a probable sheet number for the following:

Assignment #2

_____ First floor electrical plan

_____ First floor architectural plan

_____ Perspective view of building

_____ Enlarged restroom plan

_____ First floor furnishings plan

_____ Overall building sections

_____ Second floor structural plan

_____ Second floor furnishings plan

Name:

_____

Assignment #3

A. The sheet number is typically located in the _____ of the drawing sheet.

   a. upper left corner.   b. upper right corner.

   c. lower left corner.   d. lower right corner

B. List important information to be included in the title block.

_____

_____

_____

_____

C. On the following diagrams, illustrate the two most common locations of title blocks on a drawing sheet:

The final drawing set will be on 24″ × 36″ paper.

1. Show the 24″ × 36″ sheet scaled down onto an 8¹/₂″ × 11″ sheet of white paper. Include title block and space for notes on each sheet.

2. Reproduce the 8¹/₂″ × 11″ sheet as many times as necessary to create the mock-ups for a set of drawings with the components listed in the General Scenario described at right.

3. Create a mock-up set of drawings for the General Scenario of work.

Assignment #4

General Scenario for Mock-Up Set

You have created a design for the remodel of an existing loft space (40′ × 40′ × 14′ high). In order to begin the construction documents phase of the project, you must understand how many elements will be involved on the drawing set. You have determined that you will need to include the following elements in order to fully represent the design to contractors.

Demolition Plan (¹/₄″ = 1′-0″)

Construction Plan (¹/₄″ = 1′-0″)

Reflected Ceiling Plan (¹/₄″ = 1′-0″)

Finishes Plan (¹/₄″ = 1′-0″)

Furnishings Plan (¹/₄″ = 1′-0″)

(4) 40′ x 14′ high Interior Elevations (¹/₄″ = 1′-0″)

(4) Ceiling Details (Each of these will occupy approximately 6″ × 6″ on the actual sheet.)

(4) Partition/Construction Details (Each of these will occupy approximately 6″ × 6″ on the actual sheet.)

Finish Schedule (Allow 6″ high × 9″ wide on the actual sheet.)

Furnishings Schedule (Allow 9″ high × 9″ wide on the actual sheet.)

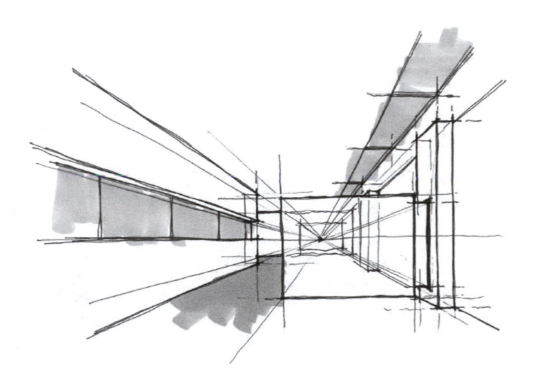

INTERIOR CONSTRUCTION DOCUMENTS **WORKBOOK**
CHAPTER 3
Communication of Intent

CHAPTER 3
Communication of Intent

Construction documents facilitate communication of the full design intent in a manner that allows the project to be priced accurately and constructed or assembled to achieve the intended result. Preparation of the construction documents, then, is focused on that communication. Communication of the design intent is reinforced by each component of the construction documents—each of the drawings, each schedule, and each part of every specification.

The position of walls or other objects, the appearance of a ceiling, the size and construction of a lighting cove, and the placement and appearance of trim around a doorway represent the type and variety of design decisions communicated through construction documents.

An important part of the communication of the design is in describing, graphically and with written communication, all of the important aspects of a project. Checking the construction documents to assure a consistent and accurate message is no less important.

This chapter has focused on the communication of the design intent. The design intent is communicated to the client by way of sketches and/or renderings and/or three-dimensional models during design phases of the project. These depictions are supplemented by floor plans. This representation becomes an agreement between the client and designer of what the project will be. It is the role of construction documents to communicate this agreed-upon design so that it may be built and meet client as well as designers' expectations.

Name:

_____

Forging a strong link between design idea and constructed product becomes the role of construction documents. Select a recent project you have designed and complete the following.

Place a three-dimensional depiction (perspective or isometric) of an aspect of the project on this page to the right.

Assignment #1 - Page 1

Describe in words (and with graphics if desired) the design decision-making foundation of the project you have selected. Use the space to the right to write or draw this description.

This description may be a conceptual basis, a theme, style, or some other impetus that helped you make particular design decisions during the project.

Assignment #1 – Page 2

Select one intersection. This may be of walls, or walls with other planes, or another intersection circumstance. Sketch it in plan and three dimensions in the space to the right. Use descriptive notes to identify materials and attributes of the design.

Assignment #1 – Page 3

For the same circumstance shown on page 3 of this assignment, illustrate another solution for accomplishing the same intersection. Show the plan and three-dimensional sketch to describe this solution. Use notes to describe materials.

Assignment #1 – Page 4

Name:

_____

Form groups of 4 in class. Each of you will take turns as the "designer" for the following exercise. Come to class with an "object" (be sure to conceal it from view) and a sketchpad.

Sit with your backs to each other so that no member of the team is able to see what another has drawn. The "designer" describes the object he or she brought while the other 3 teammates attempt to draw it. Teammates may not ask any questions or see the object.

Each of the 4 team members, in turn, will describe the object they brought to class while the 3 other members draw it. At the end of this exercise, layout the 3 drawings that represent a single object, alongside the object itself. Compare the results. Be prepared to discuss in class the relative successes of the verbal descriptions.

Assignment #2

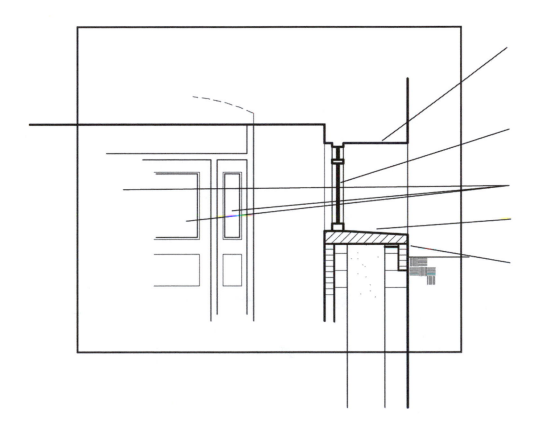

CHAPTER 4
Graphics

Graphic communication in construction documents is underscored by the quality, accuracy, and attitude of the graphics used. Items are shown on drawings with intent; they represent particular decisions made. Those reading the drawings will see only what is shown. The designer must be sure that what is shown is also what is meant. The use of proper symbols, line weights, and drawing conventions will ensure that what is *intended* to be understood by those reading the drawings is what is *actually* communicated.

Nothing about a construction drawing is arbitrary. Everything is illustrated to communicate a decision or a condition of the project. There are drafting conventions and symbols that are commonly used in this communication. Standard symbols are used to convey particular choices and decisions within each discipline, whether interior design and architecture, mechanical, electrical, or structural. Designers must be proficient in the use of proper architectural symbols in creating construction documents. They must also understand the basic symbols used by other disciplines to ascertain the precise meaning of consultants' work.

Symbols used for graphic depictions and for cross-referencing must be consistent throughout the drawings. Abbreviations must also be used consistently. The consistent approach to symbols and abbreviations assures clearer communication and less potential for mistakes or misunderstandings.

Line weights are used to reinforce the drawing intent both at a glance and upon closer inspection. Differentiation in line weights may be achieved with the employment of three categories of line weights. The three categories of line weights are used together on a drawing to communicate the range and depth of information included.

Each category of line weights has unique characteristics that separate it from any other category. Lines have characteristics that associate them with a particular cate-

NOTES:

gory and allow them to be distinguished from any line in any other category. Depending on the drawing type, whether plan, elevation, or section, each category of line weight is used consistently to communicate particular features regarding the construction of design intentions.

A consistent approach must be taken to the full complement of graphics used in a set of construction documents. Because meaning is gained through the use and combination of symbols and line weights, consistency in the use of each ensures that a coherent message is sent.

Name:

_____

Review the chapter for discussion regarding various methods of assigning line weights using AutoCAD. Then complete the assignment described to the right.

Assignment #1

Included on the CD-ROM are AutoCAD drawings in the form of .dwg files. Open the files and assign appropriate line weights to each of the lines. You will need to create new layer categories. Use the method of your choice to assign the line weights. Plot out the resulting drawings to 11″ × 17″ paper. Save the file to a disc. Place your name on the plots and the disc, and turn them in to your instructor.

Name:

_____

Individuals or firms may personalize the three categories of line weights discussed in the chapter text.

In this assignment, you will develop a scale within each of the categories of line weights. Develop a scale for hand drafted work and one for AutoCAD line weight assignment. Remember, each line in a category should be distinct from any line in another category.

Assignment #2

A. Create a new drawing in AutoCAD, with limits of 11" × 8½". Create three boxes aligned horizontally on the page, one for each of the line weight categories. Label each of the boxes as Pattern Lines, Object Lines, and Profile Lines. Create two lines in the Pattern and Profile box and three lines within the Object box. Assign a line thickness to each of the lines, and write the thickness of each line within the category. Assign a color (use the standard colors) to each of the lines, and note the color on the line. Place your name in the lower right corner, and plot the page.

B. Within the boxes on the next three pages, create your scale of line weights for each of the categories. Create two sets of vertical and horizontal lines in the Pattern and Profile boxes, and three sets of vertical and horizontal lines within the Object category box. Record the hardness and thickness of lead used to create each line. Review the chapter text for suggested ranges of leads associated with each category.

Assignment #2B Pattern Lines

Name _____

Assignment #2B Object Lines

Name _____

Assignment #2B Profile Lines

Name _____

Name:

_____

The plan at the right and the elevations on the following page describe the same object. For each of the images, indicate the lines that should be pattern lines with red, those to be object lines with blue, and those to be profile lines with green.

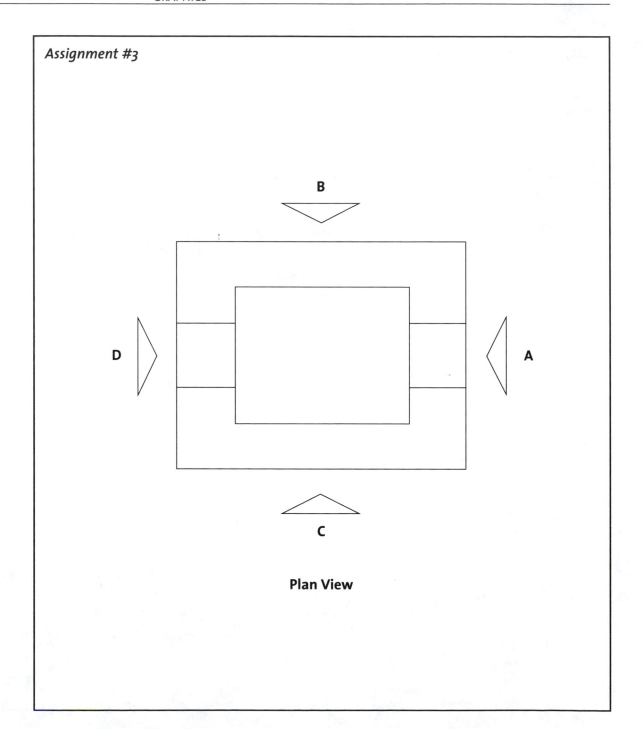

Assignment #3

Plan View

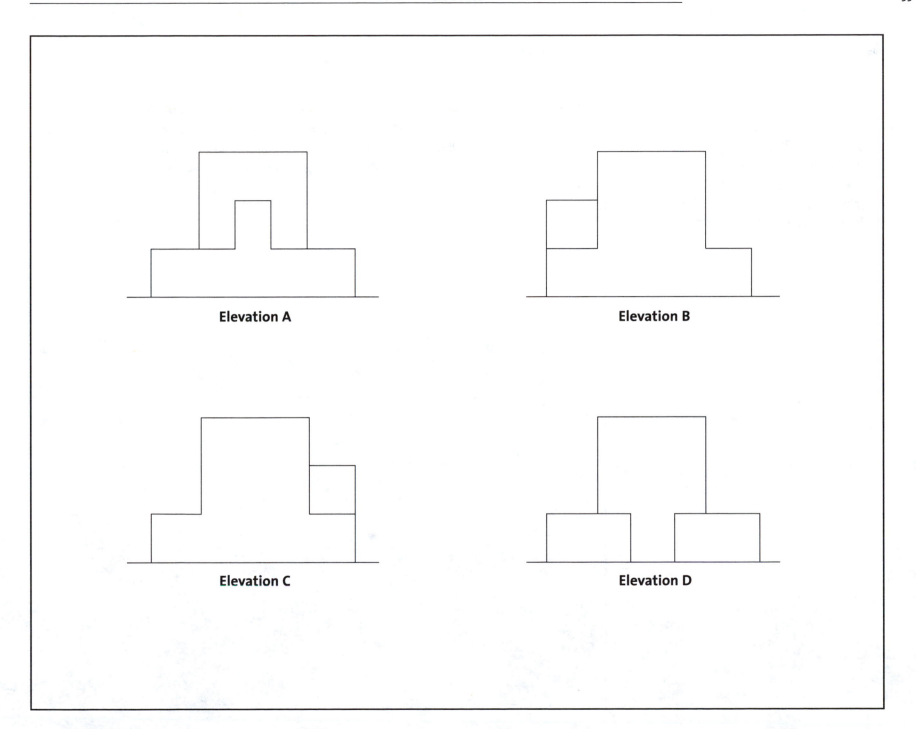

Elevation A

Elevation B

Elevation C

Elevation D

Name:

_____

Review the chapter for discussion regarding various line weights used in plan and elevation drawings. Using the lines from your developed scale of line weights in each category, complete the assignment described to the right.

Assignment #4

Select a small project you have previously designed and for which you created a plan and elevation drawing. With 8 $\frac{1}{2}$″ × 11″ 1000H vellum, overlay and trace the drawings or a portion of the drawings that will fit on the sheet. Use lead and appropriate line weights from the three categories. Place your name in the lower right corner of the tracings.

PART 2 – PRODUCTS
2.1   MATERIALS

A.   General: Provide materials that comply with requirements of the AWI quality standard for each type of woodwork and quality grade specified, unless otherwise indicated.

B.   Wood Products: Comply with the following:
    1.   Hardboard: AHA A135.4.
    2.   Medium-Density Fiberboard: ANSI A208.2, Grade MD and MD-Exterior Glue.
    3.   Particleboard: ANSI A208.1, Grade M-2 and M-2-Exterior Glue.
    4.   Softwood Plywood: DOC PS 1, Medium Density Overlay.
    5.   Hardwood Plywood and Face Veneers: HPVA HP-1.

C.   Thermoset Decorative Overlay: Particleboard complying with ANSI A208.1, Grade M-2, or medium-density fiberboard complying with ANSI A208.2, Grade MD, with surface of thermally fused, melamine-impregnated decorative paper complying with LMA SAT-1.

D.   Clear Float Glass for Doors: ASTM C 1036, Type I, Class 1, Quality q3, 6 mm thick, unless otherwise indicated.

E.   High-Pressure Decorative Laminate: NEMA LD 3, grades as indicated, or if not indicated, as required by woodwork quality standard.

CHAPTER 5
Specifications Relationship

Specifications are written to describe the details of the materials to be used, delivery and storage for those materials, installation methods, and acceptable workmanship for installation. Specifications work in concert with the graphic information presented on the drawings. While information on the drawings and schedules may identify a product in a general manner, the specifications provide depth of information. Together with the drawings and schedules, the specifications provide a clear and complete description of the scope and quality of work to be accomplished for the successful completion of the project.

The project manual contains descriptions of the bidding requirements, bidding forms, contract forms, conditions of the contract, as well as the specifications. The intention of providing all of this information is to create a description of not only the project to be constructed or installed but also a description of the *process* that will be followed in the selection of contractors and the required contracts that will bind the contractor and owner in the project.

Depending on the scope of project and the method of awarding the contract (negotiated or bid), the specifications will be written in one of many standard forms. There are four basic types of specifications: performance, reference, proprietary, and descriptive.

Regardless of the type of specification written, the individual specifications typically follow a prescribed organization. This organization allows information to be clearly and consistently presented. Generally, information in a specification is presented in a three-part format, developed by the CSI.

The first category within the three-part format is the General Requirements part of the specification. In the General Requirements portion, the scope of the section is delineated, warranty requirements are stated, and storage and handling of the product are addressed. Any general information to be communicated about the particular specification is placed here.

NOTES:

_____

_____

_____

_____

_____

_____

_____

_____

_____

_____

_____

_____

_____

_____

_____

_____

_____

_____

_____

_____

The second part of a specification regards the Products. In the Products portion, all materials and products, as well as those used to install them, are described in detail. Any tests that the product or material must pass are outlined in this portion of the specification. The way a product is to be fabricated, acceptable manufacturers, and, of course, product name or number are included here. If the designer wishes to select from a particular quality range of product, that information is also presented in the Products section.

The third part of a specification for a product or material is the Execution or Installation. In this portion of the specification, the contractor is informed of any inspections he or she must make before beginning this aspect of the project. The major aspect of this third part of a specification is exactly how the product or material is to be installed.

The construction industry has developed a 16-part format that is inclusive of all products found on any project. The CSI developed the following order of organization that is commonly used to organize the individual sections of specifications within a project manual.

Division 1-General Requirements

Division 2-Site Work

Division 3-Concrete

Division 4-Masonry

Division 5-Metals

Division 6-Wood and Plastics

Division 7-Thermal and Moisture Protection

Division 8-Doors and Windows

Division 9-Finishes

Division 10-Specialties

Division 11-Equipment

Division 12-Furnishings

Division 13-Special Construction

Division 14-Conveying Systems

Division 15-Mechanical

Division 16-Electrical

This organization provides a framework for compiling the specifications for a project within a project manual. Use of this system also allows information to be found consistently on many different project types.

Complete specifications for a project will include descriptions and requirements for every product and material used on a project. The product or material is illustrated on the drawings or called out in schedules. The specific requirements for delivery, product description, and installation are included in the specifications. Through this process, the entire set of construction documents acts as a coordinated whole.

NOTES:

Name:

_____

Each section of specifications contains general information regarding that section, the products included, and the installation parameters to be adhered to. Review the specification section included on the CD-ROM entitled "06402 INTERIOR ARCHITECTURAL WOODWORK" to answer the questions to the right.

Assignment #1 – Page 1

1. Are shop drawings required for any items of Interior Architectural Woodwork? If yes, which items are required to have shop drawings?

_____

_____

_____

2. What type of material is specified to be used for blocking and furring of the Architectural Woodwork?

_____

_____

_____

3. At what point in the project may the woodwork be delivered and installed?

_____

_____

_____

4. In which section of the specifications would information regarding wood library casework be found?

_____

Assignment #1 – Page 2

5. What is the tolerance allowed for an acceptable installation of countertops?

_____

_____

_____

6. How are wall cabinets to be installed?

_____

_____

_____

_____

7. Pencil drawer slides provided are to be rated for _____ lbf.

8. The plastic laminate cabinets to be provided must comply with which Architectural Woodwork Institute (AWI) standard type?

_____

_____

_____

Assignment #1 – Page 3

9. What is the material specified to be used as a core material for the plastic laminate countertops?

_____

_____

_____

_____

10. May integral sink bowls for the solid surface countertops be installed on the site?

_____

In which specific section of the specification have you found information to support your answer?

_____

Name:

_____

Think of a common product (it may be a piece of furniture or another product that you can readily see). Describe the product without using a brand or trade name. State the characteristics that completely physically describe the product. It may be necessary to describe the product through acceptable as well as unacceptable features. Your description must be accurate and complete enough so that the person reading your description could imagine no other product. Do not name the product you have described on this sheet. Insert the specific name of the product into an envelope and attach it to the back of this paper.

Assignment #2 – Page 1

_____

_____

_____

_____

_____

_____

_____

_____

_____

_____

_____

_____

_____

_____

Assignment #2 – Page 2

_____

_____

_____

_____

_____

_____

_____

_____

_____

_____

_____

_____

_____

_____

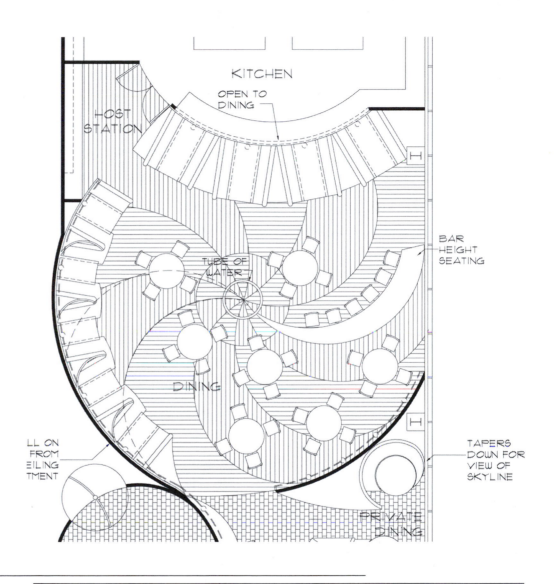

KITCHEN

OPEN TO
DINING

HOST
STATION

BAR
HEIGHT
SEATING

TUBE OF
WATER

DINING

LL ON
FROM
EILING
TMENT

TAPERS
DOWN FOR
VIEW OF
SKYLINE

PRIVATE
DINING

_____
_____
_____
_____
_____
_____
_____
_____
_____

CHAPTER 6
Plan Types and Development

Floor plans are one of the most informative drawing types of a set of drawings. They contain volumes of information regarding the project, including information related to locations of new and existing construction, ceiling features, finishes, power and communications requirements, and furnishings. From the floor plan, the next tier of drawings is referenced, such as the elevation and section drawings.

Construction plans serve as a basis for the creation of finish plans, reflected ceiling plans, furnishings plans, as well as structural, electrical, mechanical, and fire protection plans. Elevations and sections are generated from the information shown on floor plans. Floor plans must be created to illustrate the existing and future conditions, and they must be noted and dimensioned to portray an accurate picture of those conditions.

The type of information contained on each differentiates plan types. When a project scope is quite small, some of the plan types may be combined on the same drawing. Many times, for a residential remodel or addition, the demolition information is illustrated on the construction plan. On small projects, power and communications information is shown on a construction plan, rather than on a separate power and communications plan. The decision of when to show information on a separate plan is governed by issues of clarity. Of utmost importance is whether the information regarding the project is clear to those reviewing the drawings. Depending on the project's size and complexity, the types of plans commonly included on a project are the demolition plan, construction plan, finish plan, power and communication plan, reflected ceiling plan, enlarged plan, and furnishings plan.

Floor plans are generally shown by taking an imaginary horizontal cut through the space at an approximate four-foot height. Anything cut through to achieve this, such as walls, are shown with profile lines. Anything beyond, in other words, anything shorter than four feet high, is illustrated with object lines. Items located above the four-foot

NOTES:

_____

_____

_____

_____

_____

_____

_____

_____

_____

_____

_____

_____

_____

_____

_____

_____

_____

_____

_____

_____

_____

height are shown with long, dashed object lines. With this graphic language in use, the floor plan begins to take a visual dimension.

The scale selected for use in creating the construction plan is typically maintained for each of the other plan types with the exception of the enlarged plan. The enlarged plan is usually at a scale double that of the construction plan. Plans for commercial work are typically shown at $1/8'' = 1'-0''$ or sometimes $1/4'' = 1'-0''$ scale, depending on the size and type of project. For residential work, the most common scale for plans is $1/4'' = 1'-0''$, with enlarged plans often illustrated at $1/2'' = 1'-0''$.

Consultants rely on floor plans as they complete their work. Floor plans are also relied on by contractors to bid and to actually construct the project. Information on each type of floor plan must be complete, accurate, and appropriate for the scale and type of project.

Name:

Each plan type within a set of construction documents is included because it contains specific information that would not be clear if presented on another plan or drawing type.

In the matrix to the right and on the next pages, place a check mark to represent where the specific information might be located. Place a *P* in the principle location of the information.

Assignment #1 – Page 1

	Demolition Plan	Construction Plan	Finish Plan	Reflected Ceiling Plan	Power and Communications Plan	Enlarged Plan	Furnishings Plan
Existing Wall to be removed							
Attached casework and cabinetry							
Dashed lines indicating upper cabinets extending to the ceiling							
Solid lines showing upper cabinets extending to the ceiling							
Toilet to be removed							
Solid lines showing new ceiling plane							
Dashed lines showing new ceiling plane							
Dimensions of new partitions							
Glass of windows extending up to 6'-8" height							
Wall sconces mounted at 60" above finished floor (AFF)							

Assignment #1 – Page 2

	Demolition Plan	Construction Plan	Finish Plan	Reflected Ceiling Plan	Power and Communications Plan	Enlarged Plan	Furnishings Plan
Typical doors							
Door swings							
Floor material changes							
Wall material changes							
Dimensions of clear distances between furnishings							
Dimensions of ceiling planes							
Soffit dimensions							
Corridor dimensions							
Suspended acoustical ceiling grid							
Recessed downlights							

Assignment #1 – Page 3

	Demolition Plan	Construction Plan	Finish Plan	Reflected Ceiling Plan	Power and Communications Plan	Enlarged Plan	Furnishings Plan
Systems furniture							
Electrical receptacles							
Telephone requirements							
Toilet partitions							
Mirrors and restroom accessories							
Kitchen dimensions							
Restroom dimensions							
Moveable bookshelves							
Plumbing fixtures							
File cabinets							

Name:

_____

_____

Assignment #2

For this assignment select a previous project you have designed.

Locate the title block on the CD-ROM in the Chapter 6 Workbook section. Create sheets to contain each of the plan types listed below, filling in appropriate information within the title block. The scale of plans should relate to the information contained in the chapter text. Refer to previous chapters to guide you in determination of the drawing order and sheet numbering.

Plans to create:

Floor Plan

Reflected Ceiling Plan

Furnishings Plan

Enlarged Plan of a particular area.

Use appropriate line weights and symbols to create the plans. This set of plans will serve as the basis for development in future chapters.

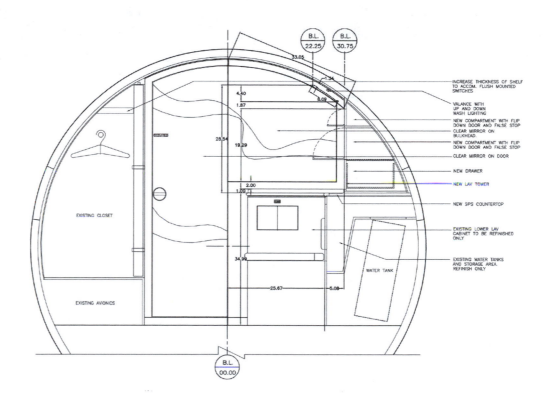

INCREASE THICKNESS OF SHELF
TO ACCOM. FLUSH MOUNTED
SWITCHES

VALANCE WITH
UP AND DOWN
WASH LIGHTING

NEW COMPARTMENT WITH FLIP
DOWN DOOR AND FALSE STOP

CLEAR MIRROR ON
BULKHEAD.

NEW COMPARTMENT WITH FLIP
DOWN DOOR AND FALSE STOP

CLEAR MIRROR ON DOOR

NEW DRAWER

NEW LAV TOWER

NEW SPS COUNTERTOP

EXISTING LOWER LAV
CABINET TO BE REFINISHED
ONLY

EXISTING WATER TANKS
AND STORAGE AREA.
REFINISH ONLY

EXISTING CLOSET

EXISTING AVIONICS

WATER TANK

B.L.
22.25

B.L.
30.75

B.L.
00.00

33.05

4.40

1.87

8.09

28.54

19.29

2.00

1.20

34.98

25.67

5.08

CHAPTER 7
Elevations and Sections

Elevation and section drawings are used to describe elements and relationships that are not entirely clear from other drawing types, such as floor plans. Elevation and section drawings are similar because relationships between vertical surfaces are illustrated and dimensioned. In addition, shapes and locations of trim, as well as the vertical locations of windows, doors, and other openings are illustrated and dimensioned. Connections to the floor, ceiling, and adjacent surfaces are illustrated as well.

Elevations

Elevation drawings end at adjacent wall, ceiling, and floor surfaces and specifically illustrate surface conditions of walls, items attached to walls, or the sides of freestanding components. Elevations are necessary to show the various finishes on walls, to illustrate ceiling shape in relation to the wall, and to show attached elements or penetrations in a wall or other vertical surface. Slicing through the space very close to the objects being shown usually creates elevation drawings.

Common elevation types include interior wall elevations, restroom elevations, kitchen elevations, casework elevations, and architectural woodwork elevations.

Elevations are drawings created to illustrate the vertical surface of something, whether that something is a wall, a piece of furniture, or a portion of an object. Sections are similar to elevations, but they go one step further and illustrate not only the surface characteristics but the construction of the bounding surfaces as well. Elevations are drawings bound on top and bottom (and, depending upon the circumstance, sides) by a single line representing the surface characteristics of the 'container,' while section drawings illustrate the actual makeup of the containers.

Section drawings are similar to elevation drawings in the depiction of vertical surfaces. The difference is that section drawings also show the construction of the wall,

NOTES:

_____

_____

_____

_____

_____

_____

_____

_____

_____

_____

_____

_____

_____

_____

_____

_____

_____

_____

_____

_____

_____

_____

floor, ceiling, or object being cut through. For existing building conditions, showing a section view represents that the designer knows the construction of the floor, walls, and ceiling and is illustrating it for the benefit of other design professionals and contractors.

Some of the common section drawings are full building sections, individual space sections, stair or ramp sections, wall sections, and casework sections.

Elevations and sections are shown at the same scale as the plan they were generated from, when they are to illustrate overall conditions. When elevations and sections are meant to illustrate more detailed conditions, they are created at an enlarged scale, often $1/4" = 1'-0"$ or $1/2" = 1'-0"$.

Name:

_____

Located on the CD-ROM is an elevation and section of a mail area. Use the provided drawings on the CD-ROM as a reference to answer the questions to the right.

Assignment #1

1. What does the diagonal hatching represent?

_____

_____

2. How wide is the filler panel strip on each side of the upper cabinets?

_____

_____

3. What is the finish material for the cabinetry?

_____

_____

4. What are the two legs that support the countertop made of?

_____

_____

5. To get more of an idea of what the countertop profile and size are, where would you look?

_____

_____

Name:

_____

The conference room elevation drawing supplied on the CD-ROM is from the same project as the mail room in Assignment #1 of this chapter. Use the information provided in each of these drawings to propose the sections marked 6/A6.1, 17/A6.2, and 18/A6.2 on the elevation. For each, create a free-hand drawing to scale, utilizing appropriate line weights, notes, and dimensions where appropriate.

Assignment #2 – Page 1

Section 6/A6.1 Sketch

Assignment #2 – Page 2

Section 17/A6.2 Sketch

Assignment #2 – Page 3

Section 18/A6.2 Sketch

Name:

_____

The section drawing shown on the CD-ROM labeled Assignment #3 illustrates a wall that is perpendicular to the floor on one face and tilted on the other face. Using the section drawing as a reference, answer the questions to the right.

Assignment #3

1. How is the wall able to be perpendicular to the floor on one side and yet tilted on the other?

_____

_____

_____

_____

2. What is the size of the recess containing the light fixture?

_____

3. Besides the angle of the wall, what do you view as the most important relationship illustrated by this section?

_____

_____

_____

_____

Name

_____

In this assignment, you will develop elevation drawings. Your instructor will assign one of the options listed to the right.

Assignment #4

Option #1
Measure each of the locations of toilet partitions, lavatories, mirrors, water closets, paper towel dispensers, tile pattern or location, and every other item located within the restroom. Use this information to create elevation views at $1/4'' = 1'-0''$. These views may be created using AutoCAD or hand drafting as your instructor requests.

Option #2
For the plans created in Assignment #2 of Chapter 6, create interior elevations of each wall surface. Illustrate and note each of the materials on the elevation. Create these elevation views with the same media as that used for Assignment #2 of Chapter 6, and place on a sheet complete with labeled title block.

Option #3
Select a kitchen to represent in elevation. Photograph the kitchen and submit the photograph with your elevation drawings. Create the kitchen elevations at a scale of $1/4'' = 1'-0''$. These views may be created using AutoCAD or hand drafting as your instructor requests.

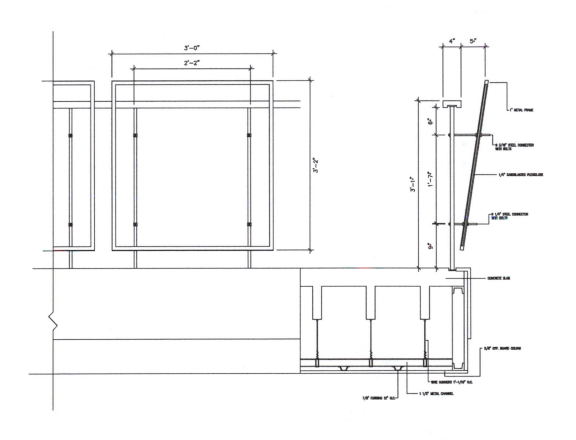

CHAPTER 8
Detail Development

Details support the design intent represented throughout the construction documents by providing an opportunity to illustrate the particular attributes of a single condition. Details provide the intricacy of information shown on drawings and are drawn at a scale large enough to suit the particular circumstance.

Details are developed and shown to communicate specific information about a particular circumstance. Details should communicate the design intentions and the functional characteristics of a particular situation. Details are shown of as many conditions as necessary to establish a consistent framework for decision making in the field.

Details may be created as plan, elevation, or section views. Occasionally, an axonometric drawing is used to best show a particular detail condition. Plan details usually show a section view of the object in question, viewing downward so that each of the components, as well as their relationship to each other, may be effectively illustrated.

Elevation details are often generated to illustrate clearances or surface relationships. Section details are used frequently in a set of construction documents. They are used to show many relationships and are important, as they articulate the relationship of the finished material to the substrate.

Standard material symbols must be used on details to ensure that each interpreter of the construction documents understands the designer's intent in the same manner. Dimensions are shown on details to accurately communicate important information, whether it is the thickness of material, distance to finished floor, or a requirement for clearance.

The scale for plan details that are aimed at illustrating more general relationships is often $3/4'' = 1'-0''$. For most interior details, a scale of $1^1/2'' = 1'-0''$ is sufficient to communicate conditions and material relationships accurately. In other cases, where intricacy of information or small items must be distinguished, a scale of $3'' = 1'-0''$ is used.

Name:

_____

From the information given on the plan and the two sections of reception desk shown on the CD-ROM, propose a detail that encompasses the transaction counter, the support for the transaction counter, and the associated area of the reception desk top/front. Illustrate a total of three iterations of the proposed detail, one per page. Each iteration is to show an increasing amount of refinement and detail decision making.

Assignment #1 – Page 1

Iteration 1 (freehand sketch at a scale of 3″= 1′-0″)

Assignment #1 – Page 2

Iteration 2 (freehand sketch at a scale of 3"= 1'-0")

Assignment #1 – Page 3

Iteration 3 (freehand sketch at a scale of 3"= 1'-0")

Name:

_____

Included on the CD-ROM is a Microsoft Excel chart for your use. Copy the table and fill in the blanks with as many questions as you can think of that will affect decisions made in detailing for the three circumstances listed here.

Assignment #2

1. Detail created for Assignment #1 of the reception desk transaction counter

2. Door frame for the entry from an enclosed interior shopping mall to a retail space

3. Lighting cove for an office corridor

Name:

_____

For the schematic three-dimensional representation shown on the CD-ROM, develop a proposed detail for your choice of the following conditions.

The detail may be hand drafted or generated on AutoCAD or another digital drafting program. Use notes to identify materials and dimensions to reinforce the graphic depiction. Create the detail at a scale of 3"= 1'-0".

Assignment #3

A. The penetration in the wall from which the transaction counter emanates

B. The relationship of the transaction counter to the reception desk (to maintain floating appearance)

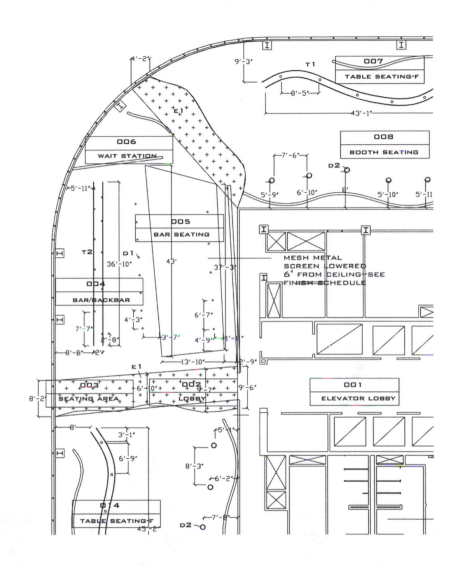

CHAPTER 9
Dimensioning

Dimensions supplement the graphic information shown on drawings in a significant manner. Dimensions locate items within space and tell the size or describe the shape of objects. They provide the intricate information necessary to manufacture, compose, and assemble elements within a project.

As in all other aspects of construction documents, accuracy, consistency, and clarity are paramount. The approach and manner of dimensioning on a project is integral to the overall quality of the set. Dimensions contribute to the overall communicative ability of the construction documents to adequately represent the designer's intentions for the project.

Each sheet of the construction document set contains different levels of information. Enlarged plans show a higher degree of detail than a floor plan; details show additional and usually more intricate information. The level of detail in dimensioning must match the level of graphic information illustrated.

Dimensions are organized in a hierarchical fashion. As dimension lines are placed further from the object, the dimensions are more general. Those closest to the object contain the most intricacy of detail.

Each line of dimensions should contain consistent information. For instance, it should contain overall dimensions, opening dimensions, or partition location dimensions.

The dimensioning text is most often placed slightly above the dimension line. The text must be visually linked to the dimension line so there is no question regarding the clarity of information shown. In order to communicate the exact intent of the drawings with dimensions, additional clarity is sometimes necessary through the use of additional terms. The most common terms are *equal, field verify, align, plus or minus, clear.*

A well dimensioned set of construction documents contains accurate and complete information. The level of dimensioning must be appropriate to the level of detail within the drawing. Dimensions must be checked for mathematical accuracy and applicability to the drawing and circumstance.

Name

For this assignment, you will use the plans developed as a part of workbook assignment #2 in Chapter 6.

Fully dimension each of the plans. Be sure to include the dimensions that are most appropriate to the particular plan type.

Assignment #1

Name

Use the plan drawing located on the CD-ROM for this exercise. With the following description, fully dimension the plan.

Assignment #2 – Page 1

Each of the four offices shown is 12'-6" × 13'-4". The hinge jamb of each door is located 7$\frac{1}{2}$" from the inside face of the adjacent wall. The width of each door is 3'-0". The "top" corner of the pod of four offices is located 2'-0" below the centerline connecting the two top columns. The bottom corner of the pod of four offices is located 6'-0" below the centerline connecting the two bottom columns. The passageway between the offices has a clear dimension of 44". There is an overhead plane in this passageway with a width of 34$\frac{1}{2}$". The overhead plane is the same length as the passageway. The office walls are not full height, and over each office is a quarter-circle suspended ceiling plane. The overhead planes will not be dimensioned on this plan.

The glazing is centered on the wall of each office. The two outer glazing panes are 30" wide, there is a 3" wide mullion, and an 82" expanse of glazing separated into four equal sections by 1" wide mullions. The walls are constructed of 3$\frac{5}{8}$" metal studs with $\frac{5}{8}$" gypsum drywall on each side.

Use the plan drawing located on the CD-ROM for this exercise. With the following description, fully dimension the plan.

Assignment #2 – Page 2

The curved segment of wall at the visual termination of the passageway has an inside radius of 115″. The center point is located 7 1/2″ towards the curved segment from the end of the passageway and is centered on the passageway. A line connecting the two termination points of the curve is parallel to and located 90″ from the outside wall of the closest offices.

A. Use AutoCAD to dimension the electronic version of the floor plan.

B. Print out the floor plan to a scale of 1/8″ = 1′-0″ on 8 1/2″ × 11″ paper. Dimension the plan using hand-drafting techniques.

An elevation and section drawing of a feature wall are located on the CD-ROM. Using the dimensions given on both the elevation and section, complete the dimensioning necessary to communicate clearly about this design.

Assignment #3

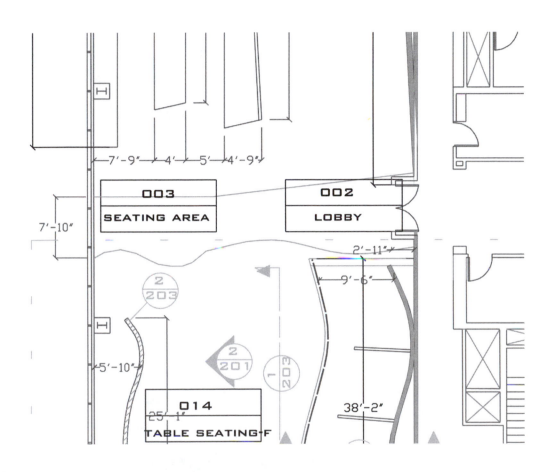

CHAPTER 10
Cross Referencing and Coordination

Construction documents are a complete package intended to fully and accurately describe the design intentions of the designer. Within this set of construction documents, the drawings, schedules, and specifications form an integrated project description. Each component within the set must be referenced to another. In addition, drawings, schedules, and specifications must be coordinated to present a coherent and consistent representation of the project.

Full and complete information about the entire project or even about one element of a project may not be gained from one drawing alone. Within a set of well-referenced documents, a clear relationship is established among all of the individual components used to describe the project. References are made from one portion of a set of construction documents to another. This reference may be made to direct the viewer to an enlarged plan for more detail, to a section or elevation drawing, or to a detail drawing. Because each drawing works in concert with the others, and with the schedules and specifications, a method of integration must be in place.

A system of referencing is made possible because each drawing on a sheet of construction documents is uniquely identified by its drawing number on the sheet and by the sheet number. Reference is made between drawings and schedules through the use of common room names, number designations, and specific designation marks. Reference is made from the drawings to the specifications through common terminology or through a specific keynoting system. Reference is similarly made from schedules to specifications through the use of common terminology.

Every cross referencing symbol has elements in common. Within the symbol, the top number or letter refers to the unique drawing designation on a sheet; while the bottom number, letter, or combination of the two refers to the sheet itself where the drawing will be found.

NOTES:

Elevation references are illustrated on a plan drawing and contain a directional indication. Section reference symbols also contain a directional indication. This is important because it tells the viewer which direction the section is "looking" to from where it is cut. The line on the symbol cuts through the elements it is illustrating. Plan details are referenced with a symbol that circles the condition to be shown elsewhere at a larger scale in a detail.

From the floor plans, references are made to wall sections, overall building sections, elevations, enlarged floor plans, plan details, and to door, window, finish, furnishings, and lighting schedules, depending on the particular floor plan.

From elevation drawings, entire wall sections may be referenced, the location of overall building sections may be referenced, and in particular, section details are called out. Elevation drawings are also referenced to door and window schedules as well as to finish schedules.

From the section drawings, section details are commonly referenced. The section details illustrate a particular condition at a larger scale. On the section drawing, the condition is seen in its overall relationship to other components and elements.

Coordination

Coordination within a set of construction documents occurs during the entire construction documents phase. The drawings, schedules, and specifications must act together to represent the full intentions of the designer to other design professionals and to the contractors. Coordination assures that each component of the construction documents is reinforcing a similar message.

Name

_____

Using the Microsoft® Excel sheet located on the CD-ROM, create symbols to fill each of the cells. Where more than one label is provided for a particular symbol, create alternative symbols for the same situation.

Assignment #1

Name

Use the plan and kitchen elevations located on the CD-ROM for this assignment. Print out the plan and elevations onto 8¹/₂″ × 11″ paper. Label each of the elevations. Coordinate the location of each of the elevations to the appropriate symbol on the plan.

Assignment #2

Furnishing Schedule

Mark	Manuf.	Desc.	Item #	Finish	Fabric	QTY
C1	Stlcase	Chr- Full, RB, BP,UA	462FFU	Stlcase pletc, blk, 4324	Design Tex Glacier, Aubergine, 1130-602	5
C2	Stlcase	Chr-Full,RB,PU	462XF	Stlcase pletc, blk, 4324	Design Tex Pharos, Wheat, 2501-102	7
C3	Stlcase	Chr-Side,Arm,Glide	1255CG	Stlcase wood, blonde on maple, full fill, 3544		13
C4	Bryt Intl	Chr-RSTA,OFN,TAB,RH	2001	Stlcase pletc, blk, 4324	Design Tex, Glacier, Steel, 1130-801	6
C5	Trnstn	Ala-carte, UP Arm, BK	TS1394	Trnstn pletc, blk, 142	Design Tex, Pharos, Wheat, 2501-102	10
C6	Trnstn	Jenny Lnge, both arm	TS3926	Trnstn wood, maple, W353	Design Tex, Glacier, Aubergine, 1130-602	2
C6a	Trnstn	Jenny, Lnge, R arm	TS3921	Trnstn wood, maple, W353	Design Tex, Glacier, Aubergine, 1130-602	1
C6b	Trnstn	Jenny Lnge, L arm	TS3928	Trnstn wood, maple, W353	Design Tex, Glacier, Aubergine, 1130-602	1
C7	Stlcase	TChr-HI,armless	453CHN	Stlcase pletc, blk, 4324	Design Tex, Glacier, Steel, 1130-801	6
C8	Stlcase	DChr-High, BK	460H	Stlcase pletc, blk, 4324	Design Tex, Glacier, Steel, 1130-801	14
C9	Vecta	Lucy, Plthm, BK	L5000	Vecta pletc, blk, PL34	Vecta Polleurathane Back, Orange, 243	10
C10	Trnstn	Crsh Can, SML	TS3366		Trnstn felt, red, 097	6
C11	Vecta	Lounge, LG, armless	F6900	Vecta pletc, blk, PL34	Design Tex, XTreme Cond, Citrus, 247-201	1
D1	Custom	Recept Desk- Stnlss Stl/ Wood	Custom	Stlcase wood, blonde on maple, full fill, 3544		1
D2	Stlcase	Walden Suite, BLT,RH	GBTS3R	Stlcase wood, blonde on maple, full fill, 3544		1
D3	Stlcase	Paladin Suite, BLT,RH	B563LD	Stlcase wood, blonde on maple, 3544		1
D4	Stlcase	Monarch Suite, DBL PED	MDPS1	Stlcase wood, blonde on maple, full fill, 3544		2
DT1	Mayline	Drafting TBL 30"x36"	M-2941	White top, 60		8
F1	Stlcase	Lat File 3'6"/ 4H	TS442L	Stlcase paint, Fog, 7236		1

CHAPTER 11
Schedules and Legends

Schedules show vast amounts of information in a highly organized manner. Schedules are coordinated and relate to both the drawings and the specifications within a set of construction documents.

Schedules provide a valuable tool in the organization and communication of large amounts of information. A schedule refers to a tabular arrangement of information. Schedules are used to provide a more in-depth understanding than can be shown on the drawings, but they are not intended to replace specifications. Schedules often serve as a bridge between drawings and specifications.

Several types of schedules are commonly used on projects. These include Finish Schedules, Door Schedules, Window Schedules, Lighting Schedules, and Furnishings Schedules.

Schedules are often sketched out towards the beginning of the construction documents phase. In many cases, the schedules have been created during the design process to organize information, to assist in presentations, and for cost estimating purposes. These initial schedules may be formalized, or they may be brief in their preliminary form. Schedules created early in the project are helpful in finalizing those decisions made during design phases of the project.

Schedules work in unison with other components of the construction documents set, namely the drawings and the specifications. Schedules relate to the drawings through symbols illustrating the precise location of an item, as well as its relationship to adjacent components or the overall project. Schedules relate to the specifications in that they describe the product in general terms. The relationship of schedules to the drawings and specifications must be well planned and consistent so that the information presented is not contradictory or absent.

NOTES:

_____

_____

_____

_____

_____

_____

_____

_____

_____

_____

_____

_____

_____

_____

_____

_____

_____

_____

_____

Legends

Legends provide a key to symbols used on a drawing. Legends relate directly to the drawing at hand. Legends provide graphic clarity to a drawing by illustrating and explaining specific symbols utilized.

Legends are used to explain symbols utilized on drawings. Legends are placed on each drawing they relate to. Other disciplines also show legends on their drawings. These legends make a designer's task much easier when searching for information on drawings. Mechanical, electrical, and plumbing drawings commonly contain legends of the symbols used. Fire protection drawings similarly contain legends. Incorporation of legends on these consultants' drawings ensures consistent interpretation of the drawings.

Name

_____

Utilizing the notes to the right, create a completed Finish Schedule, selecting one of the forms located on the CD-ROM.

Assignment #1 – Page 1

Designer: I'd like you to consider a granite tile in the entry foyer of the building.

Client: Would it be a black surface? I'm worried about dried soil showing on the surface.

Designer: I have in mind a speckled gray. The body is a medium warm gray and throughout is varying specks of dark gray and black.

Client: Ok, that sounds good. What would you recommend for the base in that space?

Designer: A 4" granite base, the very same granite as the floor surface.

Client: Now, remind me what the walls are in that room?

Designer: The north wall is a gypsum drywall, smooth finish, painted surface and is the wall with the opening to the elevator lobby. The east and west walls are glass, at least above the base. I'd like to see the granite be used as the sill for the glazing. The glazing extends entirely to the ceiling level, as you recall in our conversation last week. And, of course, the south wall contains the entry doors. Surrounding the doors, the wall surface is once again gypsum drywall, smooth and painted.

Client: Thank you. Now, I seem to recall that the ceiling is fairly nondescript in that room.

Designer: Nondescript? Actually, the ceiling seems to float. There is a cove surrounding the space and a suspended, wood paneled ceiling hangs at a 10' height.

Assignment #1 – Page 2

Designer: Let's move into the elevator lobby with our discussion. I'd particularly like your approval on the finishes in this space. With two elevators adjacent to each other on the east wall, we have mostly the elevator doors to contend with. We see those elevator doors punctuating a rich wood paneling. A grid is apparent in the wood through the 1/4" recesses. Those recesses will be painted black, so it will appear as though the wood panels are raised from the wall surface. The elevator doors are a brushed nickel finish.

Client: Sounds wonderful. How does that wall surface relate to the others in that lobby? And for that matter, what do you have in mind for the floor?

Designer: I'm glad you asked! Directly across from the elevator doors, we have designed a sculptural image that is derived from your company logo. We feel this image can be reinforced throughout the building. The material of the sculpture is brushed nickel to coordinate with the elevator doors. The sculpture will be set against a backdrop of a smooth wall painted with a matte, almost velvety finish. Each of the north and south walls will have the same finish. The flooring continues to be the same granite as the entry foyer.

Client: Ok, this sounds perfect.

Assignment #1 - Page 3

Designer: The ceiling in this elevator lobby will be a grid of brushed nickel. The grid will be reflective of the wall grid, with additional levels of hierarchy, and the materials will tie the space together. Lighting will emanate from above the metal grid and will focus on the sculpture as well as highlight the elevator doors.

Client: I'll look forward to our next meeting.

Designer: I will too and will have my assistant prepare a finish schedule for the remaining spaces we're working on. At our next meeting, you'll see the finishes we discussed today reflected in the finish schedule, and we will propose the remaining finishes as well.

There are several additional spaces included in this project. You have been asked to propose finishes for each and reflect your choices in a Finish Schedule.

The additional spaces include: Employee Break Area, Mail Room, Conference Room, Reception Area, Open Office Space.

Name:

_____

In the appropriate spaces to the right, create a legend for each of the following circumstances.

Demolition Plan: show "existing walls to remain" and "existing walls to be removed."

Partition Plan: show three different partition types, in addition to "existing walls."

Reflected Ceiling Plan: show "recessed can," "speaker," "2′ × 2″ recessed fluorescent," "pendant."

Assignment #2

Demolition Plan

Partition Plan

Reflected Ceiling Plan

CHAPTER 12
Future Trends

We exist in a time of rapid change. Change occurs at the speed with which technology transfers information. Change also occurs in the size and form of that technology. In the last 25 years, we have seen the design industry embrace increasingly intuitive and more powerful software to assist in the representation of construction documents.

Name

_____

How do you envision the future roll of technology in interior construction documents?

Visualize a point in time 20 years hence, and describe the manner in which a project is handled from design through construction. Use a narrative form and be descriptive in your prose (500-word minimum).

Assignment #1